Legends of Rock

The ROLLING STONES

Pushing Rock's Boundaries

by Hans Hetrick

Consultant:
Meredith Rutledge-Borger,
Associate Curator
Rock and Roll Hall of Fame & Museum
Cleveland, Ohio

CAPSTONE PRESS
a capstone imprint

Edge Books are published by Capstone Press,
1710 Roe Crest Drive, North Mankato, Minnesota 56003
www.capstonepub.com

Library of Congress Cataloging-in-Publication Data
Hetrick, Hans, 1973–
The Rolling Stones : pushing rock's boundaries / by Hans Hetrick.
pages cm—(Edge Legends of rock)
Includes bibliographical references and index.
Summary: "Describes the rise to fame and the lasting impact of
the band The Rolling Stones"—Provided by publisher.
ISBN 978-1-4914-1817-8 (library binding)
ISBN 978-1-4914-1822-2 (ebook pdf)
1. Rolling Stones—Juvenile literature. 2. Rock musicians—Biography—
Juvenile literature. I. Title.
ML3930.R64H47 2015
782.42166092'2—dc23 [B]   2014023796

Editorial Credits
Mandy Robbins, editor; Tracy Davies-McCabe, designer; Eric Gohl,
media researcher; Gene Bentdahl, production specialist

Direct Quote Sources
p. 4, Bloomberg.com, February 19, 2006; p. 15, 17, Egan, Sean.
The Rough Guide to the Rolling Stones New York: Rough Guides
Ltd., 2006; p. 22, 28, Fornatale, Pete. *The Rolling Stones 50 Licks*.
New York: Bloomsbury, 2013

Photo Credits
Getty Images: Michael Ochs Archives, 10, 12, 20, Redferns/Brian
Shuel, 11, Redferns/Robert Knight Archive, cover; Newscom: akg-
images, 8, Getty Images/AFP/Caio Leal, 5, imago stock & people,
22, Mirrorpix, 14, 19, 25, 27, Mirrorpix/Ashurst, 9, Mirrorpix/King
Tom, 26, Mirrorpix/Maurice Tibbles, 16-17, Mirrorpix/Ray Weaver, 21,
Mirrorpix/T King, 15, SOLO Syndication/Daily Mail, 13, Splash News/
SWNS, 7, ZUMA Press/Keystone, 23, ZUMA Press/Waz Fotopool/Ilja
HöPping, 28

Design Elements
Shutterstock

Printed in the United States of America in
Stevens Point, Wisconsin.
092014   008479WZS15

Table of Contents

A Show to Remember

On February 18, 2006, the Rolling Stones played a live show in front of 1.2 million fans. The massive crowd squeezed into a 1-mile (1.6-kilometer) stretch of Copacabana Beach in Rio de Janeiro, Brazil.

"The best moment was 'Satisfaction.' Everyone, even those who knew no English, began jumping and singing."

—a fan on Copacabana Beach, February 19, 2006

Few rock 'n' roll bands have accomplished as much as the Rolling Stones. The band has sold more than 200 million **albums** worldwide. Eight of the Stones' albums in a row went to Number One on the *Billboard* charts. The Rolling Stones have played more than 2,000 live shows. Their tours regularly break records for attendance and money earned. For 50 years they have sold out the biggest stadiums in the world. It's no surprise that people around the world believe the Rolling Stones are the greatest rock 'n' roll band in the world.

album: a musical recording that includes a collection of songs

Fans crammed together on Copacabana Beach for a 2006 Rolling Stones show.

The Rolling Stones Top 10 Picks

1 "(I Can't Get No) Satisfaction" (1965)
2 "Gimme Shelter" (1969)
3 "Paint It Black" (1966)
4 "Sympathy For The Devil" (1968)
5 "Street Fighting Man" (1968)

6 "Tumbling Dice" (1972)
7 "Start Me Up" (1981)
8 "Wild Horses" (1971)
9 "Get Off of My Cloud" (1967)
10 "Jumpin' Jack Flash" (1986)

In the Beginning, THERE WAS RHYTHM & BLUES

1

The story of the Rolling Stones begins on a Dartford, England, Railway Station platform in 1961. Keith Richards and Mick Jagger were college students taking the train into London for classes. One day Keith spotted Mick strolling through the station. Keith and Mick had grown up in the same neighborhood. They hadn't seen each other in years, so they stopped to have a chat.

Keith was shocked to find a stack of rhythm and blues albums under Mick's arm. Like Mick, Keith was obsessed with rhythm and blues, or R&B.

Backstage Pass:

Keith Richards

Born: December 18, 1943, in Dartford, England
Instrument: guitar
What he brought to the group: Keith is the heart and soul of the Rolling Stones' sound and songwriting. He is not a flashy guitar player, but he plays with remarkable timing and taste.

A school photo from 1951 shows Mick (circled left) and Keith (circled right) with their classmates.

"He's got every record Chuck Berry ever made and all his mates have too, they are all rhythm and blues fans, real R&B, I mean ... Jimmy Reed, Muddy Waters, Chuck, Howlin' Wolf, John Lee Hooker, all the Chicago bluesmen, real lowdown stuff, marvelous..."

— Keith Richards referring to his meeting with Mick in a letter to his Aunt Patty

The Perfect Musical Match

R&B is a style of African-American music. It was popular in American cities in the 1940s and 1950s. R&B is known for heavy, driving rhythms and a simple, yet powerful delivery. R&B came from jazz and blues and later gave birth to rock 'n' roll.

Rock 'n' roll was popular in England in 1961, but R&B was almost unknown. It wasn't sold in most record stores. It wasn't played on the radio.

Mick and Keith were more than just dedicated fans of R&B. They were also ambitious young musicians. Mick sang and played harmonica. Keith played guitar. They were a perfect musical match.

Keith Richards (left) with Mick Jagger (right)

Backstage Pass:

Mick Jagger

Born: July 26, 1943, in Dartford, England

Instruments: vocals, harmonica, guitar

What he brought to the group: Mick is a powerful songwriter, famous for his clever lyrics. His energy and charisma on stage are unmatched. Mick's tremendous skill on the harmonica is often underrated.

American Blues singer
Muddy Waters was
one of Mick and
Keith's musical heroes.

Rhythm & Blues School

Despite R&B's lack of availability, a small group of passionate R&B lovers thrived in London. In 1962 Alexis Korner started a weekly R&B night at the Ealing Club in West London. Korner played guitar in London's best R&B band, Blues Incorporated. During R&B night, Korner invited musicians to come up on stage and play. Mick and Keith became regulars on the Ealing Club stage.

Mick and Keith became friends with another Ealing Club regular, Brian Jones. Brian shared Mick and Keith's musical passions. The three young musicians decided to pursue their passion together.

They moved into a cheap, dirty London apartment and dropped out of college. Instead of getting jobs, they focused on their music. Every day they studied the recordings of Muddy Waters, Bo Diddley, Chuck Berry, and other great R&B artists. When they weren't listening to records, they were practicing and sharpening their musical skills.

Backstage Pass:

Brian Jones

Born: February 28, 1942, in Cheltenham, England

Instruments: guitar, keyboard, harmonica, sitar, tamboura, dulcimer, xylophone, and marimba

What he brought to the group: Brian was a natural-born musician. He could create beautiful sounds with almost any instrument. His ability as a multi-instrumentalist helped create the Rolling Stones' unique sound.

Alexis Korner was at the forefront of London's R&B scene in the 1960s.

The Rolling Stones Are Born

Mick, Keith, and Brian played their first public show on July 12, 1962, at the Marquee Jazz Club. Blues Incorporated had been scheduled to play, but the band had to cancel. The three young musicians were asked to fill the slot. As the oldest in the group, Brian became the leader. He led their musical direction, set up shows, and promoted the band. When asked for the band's name, the first thing that came to mind was a Muddy Waters song called "Rollin' Stone." And the Rolling Stones were born.

The Stones cemented their classic lineup shortly after their first show. The band brought in Bill Wyman to play bass. Then they set their sights on drummer Charlie Watts. But they would have to wait. Charlie was one of the best drummers in London. He didn't play unless he was paid. The band went through a number of drummers. But as soon as they could afford Watts, the Stones brought him into the band.

Rolling Stones, 1962; from left to right:
Charlie, Bill, Mick, Brian, and Keith

Charlie Watts

"we starved ourselves to pay for him! literally."

–Keith Richards remembering how the band paid for Charlie Watts' salary

Backstage Pass:

Charlie Watts

Born: June 2, 1941, in
Neasden, England
Instrument: drums
What he brought to the group:
Charlie was a trained jazz
drummer who could play
almost any style of music.
His tremendous skill allowed
the Rolling Stones to be
musically adventurous.

Backstage Pass:

Bill Wyman

Born: October 24, 1936, in
Lewishham, England
Instrument: bass guitar
What he brought to the group:
Bill was the oldest and most
unlikely Rolling Stone. He was
modest and quiet. He kept a
rock solid beat and had great
chemistry with Charlie Watts.

2 The Beatles vs. The Rolling Stones

Playing at the Station Hotel

In February 1963 the Rolling Stones began playing regularly at the Station Hotel. Within two months attendance at the shows jumped from 30 to more than 300. Word of the Stones' powerful, fiery brand of R&B spread through London. Soon journalists, record label executives, and even the Beatles came to see the Stones.

The most important person to see the Stones at the Station Hotel was Andrew Loog Oldham. Oldham had worked as a publicist for Brian Epstein, the manager of the Beatles. He paid close attention as Epstein transformed the Beatles into the most popular band in England. Oldham was only 19 years old, but he was brilliant and ambitious. Just three days after Oldham saw the Stones at the Station Hotel he was their manager.

Andrew Loog Oldham

A 1964 performance of the Rolling Stones

"when I heard them play I realized this was what my life was all about."

-Andrew Loog Oldham

Oldham Gets to Work

When Oldham became manager of the Rolling Stones, the Beatles were becoming superstars. Their songs were cruising to the top of the charts. Thousands of screaming fans were buying tickets to Beatles shows. Oldham used the Beatles' success to drive the Rolling Stones to their own superstardom.

Oldham approached Dick Rowe at Decca Records for a recording contract. Rowe had let the Beatles slip through his fingers. Oldham convinced Rowe that he would be making the same mistake twice if he rejected the Rolling Stones. Rowe couldn't refuse.

In just a few months, Oldham secured a recording contract for the Stones. The Stones' contract with Decca was better than the Beatles' contract with EMI Records. Oldham made sure that the Stones owned their master tapes. That meant Decca Records could never tell the Stones what songs to record or release. The Stones had complete creative control over their work.

"DICK ROWE
should be
remembered
not as the
man who
turned down
the Beatles
but the man
who signed
the Rolling
stones,"

—Andrew Oldham's persuasive
argument to Dick Rowe to sign the
Rolling Stones

Fans crowd the stage at a
1964 Rolling Stones concert.

The Bad Boys

Manager Brian Epstein helped the Beatles create a good-natured image. The Beatles were nice boys. They sang sweet songs titled "I Want to Hold Your Hand" and "Love Me Do." They were charming and witty in interviews.

Oldham took the Rolling Stones in the other direction. He helped them create a rebellious image. The Stones were the bad boy alternative to the Beatles. They had scruffy hair and bad attitudes. They sang songs titled "It's All Over Now" and "Honey, What's Wrong?" They didn't even try to be charming in interviews.

Oldham's strategy worked. The Rolling Stones developed a unique identity that separated them from the Beatles—and every other band. Teenagers began to define themselves as Beatles fans or Stones fans. You could like both bands, but your heart could belong to only one.

Behind the Scenes

The Beatles and Stones rivalry was promoted in the public eye. But behind the scenes, they were very friendly. The two bands tried to schedule their album releases at different times. That way their songs wouldn't directly compete for sales.

Members of the Rolling Stones board a plane bound for New York in 1967.

Let Their Words Do the Talking

Oldham realized the Rolling Stones wouldn't last long recording old R&B songs. John Lennon and Paul McCartney of the Beatles wrote their own songs. Their skill as songwriters gave the Beatles control over the direction of the band. They didn't have to rely on outsiders for material or direction.

Oldham convinced Keith and Mick to start writing songs. Most of the early Jagger/Richards songs were ballads. They weren't

right for the Stones. However, they were able to sell a few of their early songs to other pop stars in the United Kingdom.

Mick and Keith eventually began to write songs that fit the Rolling Stones' style. The band scored a hit in 1965 with the Jagger/ Richards song "The Last Time." Later that year the Rolling Stones released the Jagger/Richards song "(I Can't Get No) Satisfaction." The song shot straight to Number One on charts around the world. The Rolling Stones quickly became international superstars.

The Rolling Stones relax
backstage before a 1967 show.

Fame and Misfortune

As Mick and Keith became successful songwriters, Brian Jones' role in the band continued to shrink. First Brian's role as band manager and promoter disappeared after they hired Andrew Oldham. Then Mick and Keith started writing songs, pushing the band in new directions. Brian wanted the Stones to stay true to their R&B roots.

"For a long time he was the most popular person in the band. Fan letters and all that, for what it's worth. It was Brian, Brian, Brian."
—Charlie Watts

Brian and Mick, 1969

But Brian's tremendous musical ability still allowed him to contribute after the Stones stopped recording old R&B songs. The albums *Aftermath*, *Between the Buttons*, and *Their Satanic Majesties Request* are packed with Brian's unique multi-instrumental work. However, Brian played very little on 1968's *Beggars Banquet* and made no contribution on 1969's *Let It Bleed*.

Mick, Bill, and Keith working in the recording studio 23

ian's Fall

y early June 1969, Mick, Keith, Bill, and
lie felt themselves moving in a different
ive direction than Brian. They told him he
ut of the band. Keith recalled that Brian
ed relieved when they broke the news to
Brian and the Stones did not share the same
al interests anymore.

n July 3, 1969, Brian was found dead.
d drowned in the swimming pool of his
home. Over the years many theories have
ed about how Brian died. But in the end,
roner ruled his death an accident.

July 5, 1969, the Rolling Stones played
concert in London's Hyde Park. In honor
n, Mick read "Adonais," a poem written
cy Shelley. Part of the poem reads, "Peace,
e is not dead, he does not sleep. He has
ed from the dreams of life." After the
eading, thousands of butterflies were
d into the air. The band then played
favorite song, Johnny Winter's "I'm Yours
Hers". It was their first concert with
replacement, Mick Taylor.

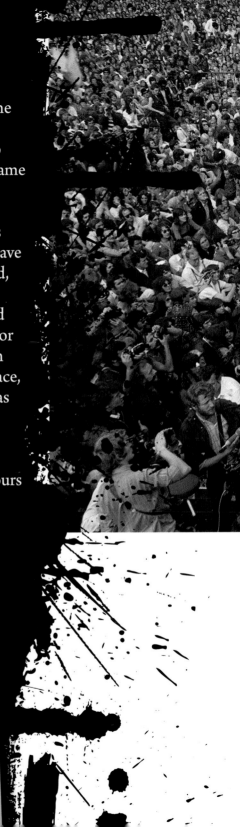

Backstage Pass

Mick Taylor

Born: January 17, 1947, in
Welwyn Garden City,
England

instrument: guitar

What he brought to the band:

Mick was a guitar **virtuoso**. In
just five years, he contributed
many of the most memorable
Rolling Stones' guitar solos.

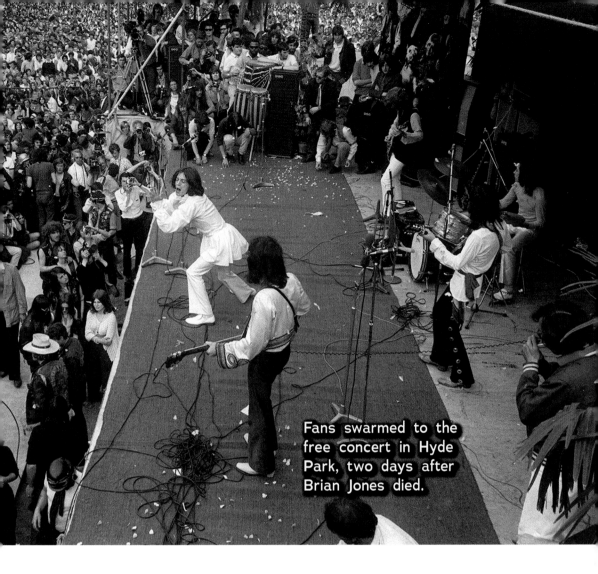

Fans swarmed to the free concert in Hyde Park, two days after Brian Jones died.

Thε Art of thε Album

Between 1968 and 1972, the Rolling Stones recorded four of rock 'n' roll's greatest albums. These were *Beggars Banquet, Let It Bleed, Sticky Fingers,* and *Exile on Main Street.* The Stones continued to win new fans. The release of a Rolling Stones album became a huge event. Fans flocked to the stores on the day of a Stones' record release to be one of the first to get the new album.

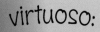

virtuoso: someone who is exceptional at playing music

⁴Life at the Top

In April 1970 the Beatles broke up. With that, the Rolling Stones became known as the undisputed greatest rock 'n' roll band in the world. Throughout the 1970s the Stones' fame and success grew to unimaginable heights. They had an army of fans. Music critics gushed over their albums. They attended parties with Hollywood actresses, famous authors, celebrated artists, and international models. No door remained closed to them. Few bands before or since have experienced the heights of fame and success reached by the Rolling Stones.

But this extreme lifestyle took its toll on Mick Taylor. By 1974 he was exhausted. Without warning, he left the band. The Stones didn't miss a beat. They hired Ron Wood, a longtime friend of the band, and recorded four more Number One albums.

Backstage Pass:

Ron Wood

Born: June 1, 1947, in
        Hillingdon, England
Instrument: guitar
What he brought to the group:
Ron fit into the band like a glove. Ron and Keith have incredible chemistry. Their guitar parts complement each other effortlessly.

A Major Rift

In the 1980s the Rolling Stones hit another rough spot. Mick Jagger and Keith Richards' relationship began to sour. In 1985 Mick released a solo album. His recording sessions for the album ran late, causing him to miss a Stones' recording session. Not only was he late, he was empty handed. He had used his best songs for his solo album.

Before the next tour, Mick sent a telegram to Keith, Ron, Charlie, and Bill. It informed them he wanted to pursue other interests. It seemed like the Rolling Stones' incredible ride was over.

Rolling Stones band photo, 1982

Rock 'n' roll Never Dies

Mick and Keith **feuded** for years, mostly through the media. In 1989 they met face-to-face and settled their differences. The band reunited. The men returned to the recording studio and made *Steel Wheels*. The album reached Number Two in the United Kingdom and Number Three in the United States. The fans were still hungry for the Rolling Stones, and the Stones couldn't wait to get back on stage. The band launched the Steel Wheels Tour. It was their first tour in seven years.

The Steel Wheels Tour kicked off a series of enormously successful world tours. Three Rolling Stones tours are among the top 10 **highest-grossing** concert tours of all time. Starting in February of 2014, the Rolling Stones launched yet another tour, the '14 On Fire tour. Most of the Stones were more than 70 years old, but they still rocked.

The Rolling Stones were **inducted** into the Rock and Roll Hall of Fame in 1989. Rock legend Pete Townshend, of the band The Who, gave the induction speech. "The Beatles were fun … " said Townshend. "But the Stones were what made me wake up." he added. "They're the only group I've ever been unashamed of idolizing." Townshend continued, "And each of them, in their own way, has given me something as an artist, as a person, and

Chart Topper

"(I Can't Get No) Satisfaction" was the rocket that shot the Rolling Stones to superstardom. The song got its start when Keith woke up in the middle of the night. He grabbed a guitar, turned on a tape machine, and recorded the unforgettable guitar **riff**. Keith gave the tape to Mick, and Mick wrote the memorable lyrics. "Satisfaction" had all the trademarks of the Rolling Stones hits that followed. It had a driving rhythm, a catchy melody, and clever lyrics.

feud: a long-running quarrel between two people or groups of people

highest-grossing: making the most money

induct: to formally admit someone into a position or place of honor

riff: a short repeated melody played on an instrument

Glossary

album (AL-buhm)—a musical recording that includes a collection of songs

feud (FYOOD)—to quarrel with another person or a group of people

highest-grossing (HYE-uhst GROW-sing)—making the most money

induct (in-DUHKT)—to formally admit someone into a position or place of honor

riff (RIF)—a short repeated melody played on an instrument

virtuoso (vur-choo-OH-soh)—someone who is exceptional at playing music

Read More

Miller, Heather. *The Rolling Stones: The Greatest Rock Band.* Rebels of Rock. Berkeley Heights, N.J.: Enslow, 2011.

Robertson, Robbie. *Legends, Icons & Rebels: Music that Changed the World.* Toronto: Tundra Books, 2013.

Tougas, Joe. *The Beatles: Defining Rock 'n' Roll.* Legends of Rock. North Mankato, Minn.: Capstone Publishers, 2015.

Internet Sites

FactHound offers a safe, fun way to find Internet sites related to this book. All of the sites on FactHound have been researched by our staff.

Here's all you do:

Visit *www.facthound.com*

Type in this code: 9781491418178

Check out projects, games and lots more at
www.capstonekids.com

Index